**Interactive Press**

## *Old Time Religion and Other Poems*

*Andrew Leggett is a poet who works as a consultant psychiatrist in private practice. His writing draws on personal experience translated into the language and structure of dreams. His work is informed by interests in contemporary mythology, psychoanalysis and art. His concerns for poetic rhythm and form contrast themselves with the context of a busy professional, personal and family life. He has also published short stories, literary reviews and papers on ethical matters.*

*He lives in Brisbane with his wife Ann. He has a daughter Angela, a son Joseph and a stepson Jack. This is his first book of poems.*

# OLD TIME RELIGION
# AND OTHER POEMS

*To Dear Pauline*
*with love*
*and best wishes,*

*Andrew L*
*22/6/98*

*(P.S. I am enjoying your*
*book very much.)*

*by*

## Andrew Leggett

*Interactive Press*
*Literature Series*

Interactive Press
an imprint of Interactive Publications
9 Kuhler Court
Carindale, Queensland
Australia 4152
reiter@powerup.com.au
http://www.powerup.com.au/~reiter

First published by Interactive Press, 1998
Copyright © Andrew Leggett

Printed in 11/13 pt Optima on Galliard by Gabba Graphics and Copy Print Xpress, Queensland, Australia. Made, printed and bound in Australia.

National Library of Australia
Cataloguing-in-Publication data:

Leggett, Andrew A. G. (Andrew Alfred George), 1962- .
Old time religion and other poems.
ISBN 1 876819 00 6

1. Title.

A821.3

For Angela, Joseph and Jack

# Acknowledgments

*Jacket design by David P Reiter of Interactive Press*
*Jacket and other artwork by Suzanne Mintel*
*Author's Photo by Ann Leggett*

*Publication credits for individual poems: Antipodes (USA), The*
*Australian, Best Of Micropress, Boardwalk, Brisbane Review, The Bulletin,*
*Canberra Times, Catalyst, Can We Hear It Again Please (UK), City Park*
*Radio Launceston, Coppertales, Earth Wings, frogpond (USA),*
*Heartland, Hobo, Imago, Iron (UK), LiNQ, Micropress, Northern*
*Perspective, Overland, Paper Wasp, Poetry Manchester, Poetry Nottingham,*
*Quadrant, Radio 92FM Hobart, Redoubt, Resurgence (UK), Scope,*
*Seriously Fishy, Sky Falling (New Zealand), Small Packages, Social*
*Alternatives, Spin (New Zealand), Southern Review, Studio, Tears In The*
*Fence (UK), Ulitarra, Unreal Estate, Verandah, Westerly, Wrapping The*
*Dragon (UK), Zuzu's Petals Quarterly On Line (USA).*

*Thanks to Gwen Harwood, Judith Rodriguez and David P Reiter for*
*critical assistance and advice on various drafts of the manuscript.*

# Contents

## Wild At Heart

## Power Of The Name

# Old Time Religion

'Sodom and Gomorrah' cried the man
who was meat between biblical sandwichboards
preaching to the seagulls and Salamanca marketers
flung like statues on the lawn.
He read from Revelation   stretched the Apocalypse
expanded the bestial   blew the last trumpet
struck a bold abomination as we munched
our spring rolls   danish cones   dagwood dogs
immune to salvation.  Blessed with a voice like
Reverend Ian Paisley and without a following
not half as dangerous.  A man who can mention
Sodom and Gomorrah twice in a sentence
is my kind of preacher.

My father used to fall asleep in church.
When the turns came on
his jaw would drop
his eyelids droop.
The air escaped him with a hiss.
He mumbled 'All right son'
each time I elbowed him
and slumped a little lower in the pew.

The bread came round — small white cubes
on a paper doily on a silver plate.
We all took one and waited
until the pastor said:
'in memory of me'
and ate together then,
remembering the broken body
and the slicer of the bread.

The thimbles full of grape juice
came in dozen trays with slots.
I took mine reverently and passed them on.
Tense, I sensed it coming.
Then he slumped.  His fingers slipped.
The small glass dropped.  The blood was spilt.
The congregation stared and rose to sing a hymn.

I WATER MY BEER
It was with a certain pride
that Kavanagh displayed the sign.
Since Jesus turned the water into wine
at Cana, no miracle had attracted
so  many thirsty witnesses.  The men
of Clement's Ridge still lined
the bar in undiminished numbers
waiting, it would seem,
like visitors at Lourdes
for a sign
of Jimmy pouring
water into beer.

She sits all day in the bus shelter
on Edward Street without any cover.
Then in the evening, she crosses over
to spend the night in the other shelter.

As he mumbles, the numbers stick in his beard
on the steps of the Astor Centre
where he sits in his trackpants, coat and jumper
guarding his bags of crumpled-up paper.

When she remembers she was a doctor,
she moves to a bench on Wickham Terrace
where the bleary blind shake tins at you:
the officially sanctioned beggars.

In the storm he is lurking in his filthy hat
behind a pillar in the car park.
The evening is full of menace.
He lives in dread of the wet.

She always carries a knife with her.
You mustn't consider consulting her.
She has been seen to go into Mozart's
to ask for a glass of water.

He is out in the open air
taking down car numbers
in a spirax notebook foraged
from the council dinner bins.

There is terror when they collide
outside the Baptist Tabernacle.
She has no knife.  He cannot see her.
Is this water spilling over his feet?

I used to be Jesus
Christ ya know
in a former life
in a better place
where the doctors
were the guardians
and the nurses
were angels.
But then they cured me,
turfed me out.
I hit the road
with my ghettoblaster
dangling like thirty
dirty silver pieces.
As you cut
my rotting carcass
down, remark
on how this Judas
clawed the bark.

From the hospital carpark
where the land falls away to a forest
chosen for housing development,
the shock of the blue September sky
makes him look up.

He is gazing at the moment of completion.
A skywriter is diving into the final 'S'
of JESUS SAVES, that final hook
like the blade of a can opener
tearing its way into heaven.

I am boarding up the windows
to keep out those lousy sparrows,
the ones that circle around the head
of that holy fool, the tramp
in the silk surplice, the one
with the pendant of Ronald McDonald,
the rollerblade boots and the tracts
by American pentecostals he says
are the words of St Francis.

I am boarding up the windows
to keep out those lousy sparrows,
the ones that twitter and rest on the hand
of that man, the filthy clown
whom the whole farmyard follows,
the man whose ruddy face glows
as he reads aloud to his mule
from the *Book of Mormon* the passage
about the Tibetan space program.

I am boarding up the windows
to keep out those lousy sparrows,
the ones that nest in the tangled beard
of that crazy scarecrow, the wizard
who claims that his skates are the chariot
Ezekiel saw when the Lord appeared
in the sky as a system of wheels
within wheels, when God sent the angels
Michael and Gabriel to bless and assist me
in boarding up the windows.

**I.**

Archbishop Dalgetty
walks in the city
carrying his sexuality
locked up safely
in a permalite briefcase.

It has taken the form
of a tightwound mainspring
in an old alarm clock.

The women in the city
are exceptionally beautiful.
Whenever one passes
she triggers the mechanism,
makes the rusty bells ring,
panicking Daigetty.

**II.**

Archbishop Dalgetty
retreats to his vestry
to direct his attention
to the problem of the split
between sex and affection.

The summer night
is ruptured
by the sound
of flying foxes

satyring desire
in the old cathedral's
mango tree.

He prays for deliverance
but he cannot resist
while the fruit bats fornicate.

He reaches for the briefcase
and opens the latches.

His pupils dilate
like a frog's
that's seen lightning.

He is taking her out today
witnessing.
She has left her statistics lecture
and is stepping out
into the Great Court
to pray.
He is a nine-digit number
somewhere.
She is using her cellular telephone.
His voice is sonorous.  He urges her
to put on the whole armour of God.
He promises eternal life.
Every pimp has his promises.
She is wearing her spiritual G-string,
her Chanel No. 5.  It is his will
that she go to the Union refectory
where a young man in black
is sitting alone with a notebook
hanging out to be hit.

The poet is shaken from his work
by her left breast overflowing his coffee cup
and the sweet breath of her mad red lips
whispering 'God loves you
and has a wonderful plan for your life.'

The regular lunchtime meeting
of the Evangelical Union Medical Cell Group
is about to take place in the Anatomy Building.
Anthony tries to look inconspicuous
as his hand sneaks up Janice's thigh
while Douglas jealous but sanctimonious
grits his teeth and slips his Gideon's
pocket New Testament into his underpants.
Andrew is humbly washing girls' feet
but Julie insists
that he lick out her toe jam.
Bored Jan and Tony sneak off
for a quick fuck during the prayer time.
Doug prays for guidance and sharpens his scalpel.
Creatively flirting across the cadaver
Julie shows Andrew
her prize dissection of protestant scrotum.

The Horned One squats
in the forest space
where he once consorted
with Diana and her sisters
in a wild unmanacled orgasmic dance
of motherlove and brotherlove
of father maiden love
himself a maiden and the maiden's child.
With hairy elbows resting on a stump
he hangs his mangy head
between his hobbled knees
and tries to pump
his lonely member with his paw
but finds himself unmanned.
These many years imprisoned
in the earthdeep world and manlocked
belt, the Goddess stirs.  The Hunter prays
that she will find her strength
in covens separate of sistermaking,
leave her monastery and join him
in the act by reaching
for his microphone and crying
in her gravel voice
'Just give me more
of that ol' time religion.'

The dreamer finds himself
at the edge of a body of water,
discarding the remains
of a dry old bunch of roses.

Each broken flower
disintegrates on contact,
smashing the meniscus covering
the drowned adultress.

The shades in the pool
are fallen stems and petals.
From the swirling waters,
the damned girl rises

as the shell of a flower,
a spunsilk goblet
with the petals settled,
fallen at the heart.

Before she woke,
he turned to her and kissed
the cracked lips of the dawn,
taking from her mouth
the eucharist of dried saliva.
He knew nothing
of its transubstantiation
to a fleshy rose
that would stick in his throat,
take root in his chest
and press its thorns
deep into the base of his skull.
His only thoughts
were of the beauty
of her fierce red acne
that blossomed in the first two months
of oral contraception
and the dull sense of relief
that it was her body
that was being broken.

A piece of charcoal in the bannock marks
him as the one.  This year everything
is his, crowned with flowers.  Last year's king
is burnt to ashes, flies up with the sparks.
This year he is free to fart at druid,
bard and vate, loving girls, priestesses, wives —
more than he's known in all his former lives.
He seeds the stars but never knows the brood.

The year is gone.  He drinks the bitter mead
the druids brewed.  The vates have bound his hands.
Bards sing his spirit to the summerlands
before Taranis' bolt falls on his head
and all the joy and all the grief are freed.
Blood seeds the earth, the harvest guaranteed.

'I'll get a woman for it next time'
sed the man and slunk me off
to mend the tail between my legs.
Well, women are warmer, more creative,
more intelligent than most.

My friend Sally lives on women's land.
Yes, a man can be a feminist, she sez.
But I'm not about to flash
my honorific badge.  My father was the first
male member of the W.C.T.U. —
(that's Women's Christian Temperance Union).
My mother was the president.
He stacked the chairs.

Always apologising for ourselves, we are
the token man at the bottom of the totem pole
beneath a heavy burden.  Isis, Ishtar,
Hecate, Ceridwen all sitting on our heads.
No room for horns on our horned god
sez my friend Pam who knows
that women worship women.

'I'll get a woman for it next time'
sed the man.  And she'll be comin'
with a woman when she comes.

The iron-masked one
chokes in his chair alone
on the word 'indifference'.
Transmitters sound it
from his granite throat.

At the medieval fayre,
the children find the jester
drowned in mud.
The sky shows mercy,
showers the world in tears.

The stone man and the fool
are buried in the church.
After bread and wine,
the children are tucked in
with a blanket of fog.

Dancing
on the table
at Club Babylon
whiskey to go
and a broken stiletto
the evangelist's daughter
has fallen
into the face
of a futures broker.

Father preaches hellfire
along the red light strip
shaking his fist
at Rock'n Roll
that contemptuous bodgie
leaning out the window
of the FJ Holden
waiting for the light
before dropping rubber

crying 'Reach for her!
Stretch and reach, old preacher man!
Extend your hands
to hold her up.
Heal the tear in heaven
where she slipped.
Extend you hands
to touch the shock
of that electric latex strip.'

the mercy sister
has the tattered habit
of leading the departed
up and down main street

i have followed her veiled skeleton
walking a greyhound
from the night owl convenience store
past the mt olivet hospice
to the edward st ferry

where a council employee
comes with scheduled regularity
to take the coins
from her hollow sockets
to take her over
to the other side

# *Caligula's New Clothes*

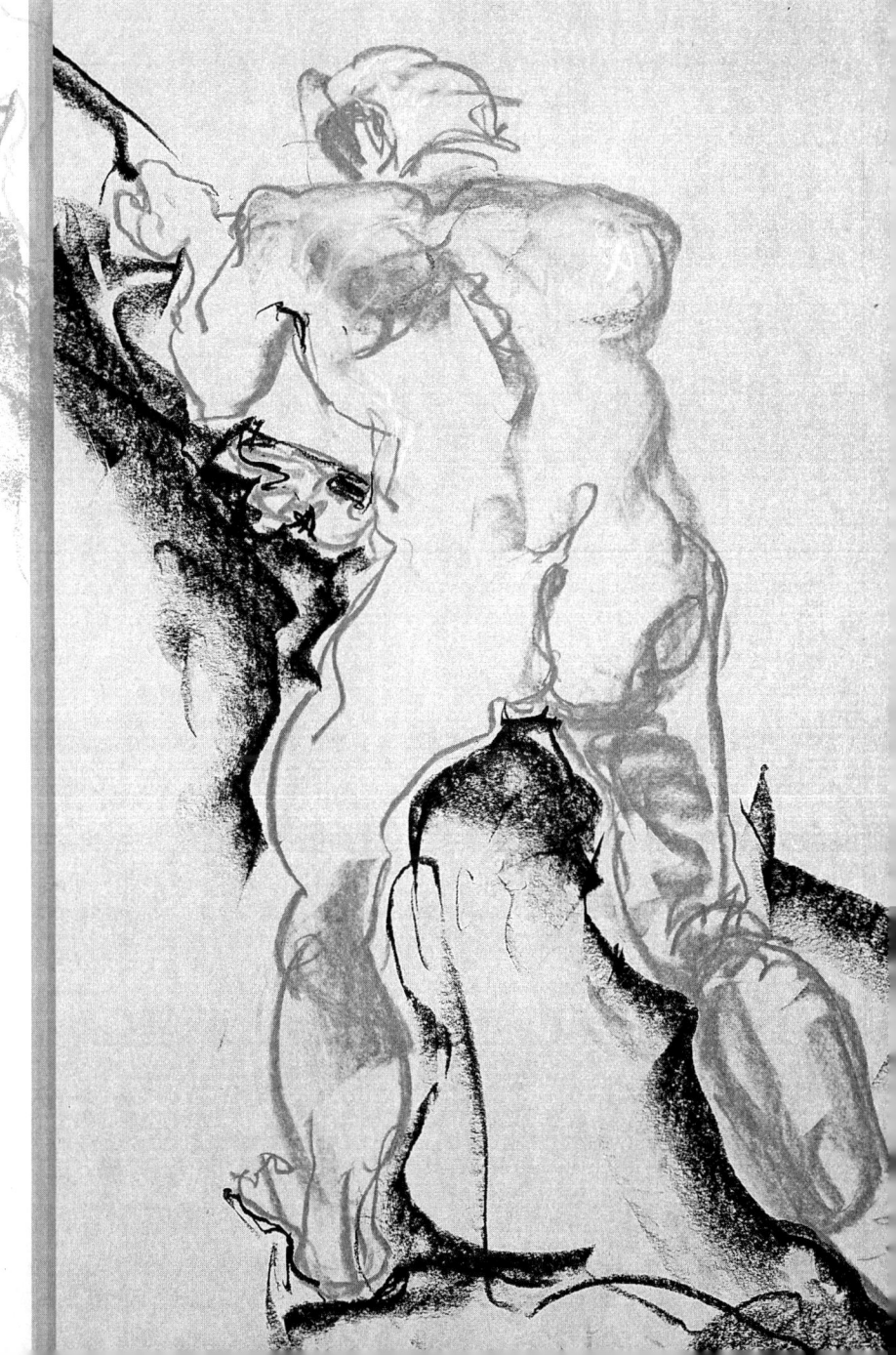

Friday nights, we conscientious students,
hanging out for premature exposure
to the sights and smells that delight a doctor,
found it all in victims of road accidents,
domestic brawls and shark attacks.  Too eager
for misery, I shed the facility
to scan reality selectively.
My efforts to shut it out were far too meagre.

An elderly coquette once beckoned me
to view her leg darkly, through a cloud of fly spray
with which the gagging nurse expunged the larvae.
The cobweb of naked veins was all that supported me
above the space consumed from the flesh by maggots.
I called my friend.  He couldn't see the maggots.

Bowen in the winter
is a tent city
with a thousand itinerant tomato pickers.

Every year
one of them blows his head off
and the doctor must identify him
as a dead thing with no name.

No one else will own the suicides
so the doctor carries them about
in his big black bag.

He has a cupboardful at home.
A treasuretrove
of half heads.

She came to us from the roadgangs,
riding into town on her bicycle,
not knowing that the bulge in her belly
was from more than beer.

A big girl
with a head like a cow,
she lived in a playground
where all could share
the swings and the seesaw
and everyone with brown eyes
was told they were beautiful.
When the waters broke,
she'd never have known
where it came from.

And when that little blue
mannequin slipped out
covered in sack,
even that wetnosed doctor,
the Brisbane boy,
agreed with me
to age the foetus
at nineteen weeks
so she'd never have to bear
a funeral.

The child the father bashed
is dead.  The wait in cas.
The resting ward.  The neuro obs.
The scan not done.  The mother
sobbed.  The bleed.

The deadened nurse has stuffed
the hole with cotton wool.
The orderly has pushed
the tray that bears the shell
the father bashed to freeze
of mortuary.  The hell.

The knife the coroner
must wield.  The photograph.
The saw.  The bold autopsy
slash.  The open skull
of fatherbashed.  The torn.
The secret of the sore.

The Daleks at the bar
are boozing and smoking
choking on their own
gas.  Their lungs are full
of carbon and their hearts
are silicon.

Daleks deal death
to interplanetary visitors
and they use strong toothpaste
so they're good
to kiss.

The Doctor says
'Daleks must be destroyed.'
but he has vested interests
in staying alive
and he's far
too rigid.

I long to see again
conveyor belts of armoured
tincans endlessly processing,
to hear again
those Dalek voices
tonelessly rejoicing
'Exterminate.  Exterminate.'
affirming my conviction
that Daleks roll their own.

The Dalek in the corner
isn't lonely. He's just dreaming
Dalek dreams of Dalek
deeds. He doesn't want you.
No. It's no good offering.
He doesn't want
to touch you. He swivels
and he spits a warning
round or two.

A Dalek in a corner
is a tight fit.

Staring into those redveined bulging eyes,
Armand was forced to recognize this thing
impaled so crudely on the metal star
of his blue Mercedes Benz SE
as the shrunken head of Jean-Pierre.

This was he, that gentle one
Armand kept chained up in the room downstairs
and shocked until he begged to share his bed
that night in the verandahed bungalow built
on the banks of the Copabanana River.

The courtyard where the Merc was parked lay strewn
with evidence from which Armand would later
reconstruct the memory of method
and the taint of culpability.
The amyl nitrate spray lay where it fell.

The shrinking pot hung suspended by a hook
above the embers of the railing timbers.
The machete lay nearby and blood
pooled on the paving stones.  In the bucket,
melted ice and the remains of Veuve Clicquot.

They had danced a wild dance that night
from the moment that Armand switched on
the old gramophone.  Satchmo cried:
'Here come Brother Higgenbotham down
the aisle with his slide trombone.  Blow it boy!'

Six days had passed into the dark
before the memory of jazz receded
into the trumpet of that damned machine.
As the table turned, the diamond needle
worn to the bakelite made scratchings

that woke him from the trance. The saints
had left their calling card.  Armand in grief
wept sober tears which moistened once again
those fragile puckered lips of Jean-Pierre.
Those lips will never blow again.

In a dark recess off Arcadia
the steps lead down from the pavement
to the world of the subterranean
establishment, Ripley's Believe It Or Not.

Our heroine, a dwarf named Elvira,
bobs her large head to the ticketseller
and descends like a tiny Persephone
warped by a hall of mirrors.

She passes through mazes of cases
of snakes, through lairs of dark creatures,
down ladders to dungeons where prisoners
cry out from the bowels of iron maidens.

Her memory unwinds like a skein of wool
guiding her back to the place of strange lights
where Ariadne cried when the thread ran out
but proceeded with nothing to guide her.

The universe contained within these walls
consists of chambers in chambers in chambers
where reality is stretched to snapping on the rack,
where the inner world reflects the outer world.

Blindly, the weird antiquities
point her way towards the case
marked COSTA NEUE VOODOO CULT
where the leather head is the centrepiece.

Elvira, standing on a packing case,
gains sufficient height to meet the relic face
to face.  Her heart leaps from her chest.
Her eyes meet eyes of disproportionate size.

Drawing her Phillips screwdriver,
she jemmies open the display and lifts the head
high by its ancient hair, kisses the eyes
and tucks it into the empty cup of her Triumph brassiere.

The suckling of those wrinkled lips
will soften the scars.
When she climbs those last stairs
her floral blouse will not disturb the tourists.

Kafka is searching
for the Kaffeehaus lavatory.

His bladder is bursting
as he reaches the door.

Kafka is thankful
that there is no queue today.

He pushes and enters
the little world
on the other side of the door.

Kafka is using
a european urinal.

He is anxious about pissing
in a place so public.

Kafka is thankful
there is no one else here today.

He finishes.
He buttons up.
He washes his hands.

Kafka looks left of him
to the lavatory cubicle.

He finds to the right of him
only the urinal.

Kafka is thankful
that the door is in front of him.

He is certain
that it was a door
when he first walked in here.

Kafka's door opens
to another empty cubicle.

He is trapped in the world
of a Kaffeehaus lavatory.

Kafka is thankful
that he has his train timetable.

He studies it
furiously
to find a way out of here.

*after Franz Kafka*

Stanley the cockroach
abandoned all ambition
on the evening he entered
the Stanley Street on-ramp.

As he crossed the three lanes
to the Turbot Street exit,
the lights in his side mirror
were those of the exterminator.

He dreamed for a moment
of impending retirement
from his job as a filing clerk
at the Department of Environment.

This lapse of attention
at the wheel of the Beetle
ended in collision
with Scientific Pest Control.

My god it's fun
exploring these stormwater drains
contriving letters
to the Brisbane City Council
telling them their pipes are cracking
sticking my head through outlets
into greater caverns
finding frilly nightwear
on the clotheslines
of Indooroopilly backyards.

Suddenly
a ragged blaster hole
explodes beside me.
I smell the blue suits
and the pounding feet.

No longer cautious of the slime
I'm splashing frenziedly
scrambling for an outlet
feet scurrying the metal rungs.
I smell the flesh below —
they're setting fire to me.
My head is punching out
the manhole in the middle of the road
and popping up between the jackboots

shining
in the streetlight
as I watch his backswing
and my chin rests on the bitumen — light

peering out between his legs.
I feel it crashing down.
My head is beating blood
across the butt of a .22.

We smashed the windows
on the night
the Governor bestowed
an honorary degree
on dear old Joh.
Despairing students
ate a ratsak meal
relented then
and washed it down
with ipecac.
Examination of
the stomach contents
brought the motive back.
The knowledge
of the retching soul
who bends beneath Silentia
the holy cistern god
and vomits in the bowl.
It takes hard work
to get to know
hard work
to hold it back.

The Emperor has ordered another parade.
Compulsory attendance on pain of death.
Here he comes now, swigging on a Carlsberg,
surrounded by all his sycophantic mates.
He could piss into a bucket and they'd drink it.
That's if those whores would give him room to aim.
The chamberlain will raise a tax to pay this rent-a-crowd.
The police are punching anyone who tries to leave
and press gangs patrol the city beach, armed with half-nelsons:
'So you thought this was just another public holiday.'
The shoulder pops and dislocates.  No one laughs
at the imperial buttocks flabbing in the breeze.
Photographers are taking rolls for Vogue.  A kid cries out:
'The king is in the nude!'  The royal hard-on droops.
They are taking the child away to put out his eyes.
The tailors' heads tilt laughing on the gibbet.

## I.

'This is the game,' Jack thought. 'These men
in their smart suits coming down the road
are our assassins. What wouldn't I give
for bubble gum, an ammunition clip, an AK47!'

Loading her pipe with a skin of toad,
the sniper on the ridge caught a whiff
of danger in Jack's thought. She lit
and drew in bufotenin. (Heavy shit.)

In all her years with special branch,
the sniper never watched a thought balloon
take such subversive form. It peeled away
this woman's skin, let the toad mind launch
its brute attack. Siting the gum balloon
above Jack's head, she blew the thought away.

## II.

'This is the game,' thought Jack, the comic
strip hero, as he stripped to the waist
rather than scrape the residue of gum
from his suit. He grabbed the hand of his atomic

blonde companion and ran. The smart suits chased
them through the jungle, stumbling at times. The drum
beat in the sniper's mind in time with the toad's
heartbeat. Jack in her sights, her eyes the toad's.

The jungle thinned.  The ground grew soft.  It gripped his feet.  The smart assassins drowned.  As Jack drew the blonde in the strip in his mind, he sank in the mire. Before he drowned, he drew a straw.  She slipped away underground with the straw to breathe through. Keeping the straw in her sights, the sniper fired.

He wakes screaming, struck by the real sound
of glass breaking, by the rush of cold air,
and by the real sound of his own scream.
His scream becomes a war cry returned for a wound
to a man's eyes.  The shattered windows stare
fire at the intruder.  There is no dream.
There is no iron to spike her, only glass,
this strange woman cutting herself with glass.

Whether she fell or was pushed, her breath stinks,
her face close to his as he lies in bed naked.
He was not born so suave as to ask what she drinks
or whether she would like to join him in bed.
He is cold and still screaming.  He does not want to meet
this girl, her head through the frame, her arse in the street.

When y're shipped up to the Derwent
to work as a registrar
they like to see a new doctor
up at New Norfick.
The social worker will walkya
up to Willow Court telling stories
about the skeletons the workers find
when every few years
they clean up the banks of the Derwent
up at New Norfick —
the wanderers that nobody missed
because of their beanies
because they wore three sets of underwear
away with the fairies.
Y'see them wandering in the grounds
and wonder which one's next.
But they've givenya the locked ward
and y'get to carry a key
big enough to fill a jockstrap
so none of yours are going wandering
among the wattle with their wild oats.

After a day at the Derwent
y're feeling the weight of that key
and things on the ward are so bad
that y'wanna let them wander
with their vacant looks
like badges saying WON'T BE BACK
GONE FISHING
But the nurse sez:

'Keep y'r instrument
in y'r pocket'
so y'hide the key
and let the nurse
unlock the door.

In a Salamanca gallery,
the alchemist discovered Aaron's rod.
The craftsman fashioned it
from native antipodean oak
grown on an island sacred
to the desolation of the Snake.
The rod is frozen
in the act of transformation.
The snake winds in oak
towards the neck of the staff
like a system of veins
towards the neck of femur
which spins in its socket —
an axis mundi
frozen in the Dreaming
when the Rainbow Serpent's blood
congealed in circles
and the British came.
With this stolen magic bone
White Melchior has sung to death
the firstborn race
and brought dishonour
to this honest snake
which I now claim.

There is an old killing in the place
and he is drawn up the gully rockhopping.
The afternoon is failing as he jumps
between the trunks of fallen eucalypts
and limestone outcrops. Cicadas
and the gumflowers fill the air
with scent and roaring. He stumbles
at a landfall, missing the ledge.
Both knees are grazed. Below
the wallaby people are making their dreaming
in the clearing on the high kikuya.
The light is failing and the dew is settling
on the skin of the intruder. Somehow
he is spared.

Later that evening, she is driving.
He is drawn too late to warning
as the wallaby blind in the high beam lights
jumps at the bumper of the green Charade.
The warclub thuds, the car
skidding across the road before braking.
The air is full of animal rubber fear.
She and the beast are whimpering.
The wallaby has smashed a femur.
He takes the wheel and ploughs
the front wheel drive from first to reverse
from reverse to first again
across the neck he loves.
He is killing his dreaming.

*for Daniel Yock, dancer who died in police custody*

Forgive me, gubber [1]
for swinging a fence paling
dangerously close to your guilt.
Fourex is slower
than byebye damper [2]
at the Boundary Hotel
where us blackfellas queue
to pay for our poison.
You trained us, gubber.
For the sake of the brewer
you let this picaninny
grow to a dancer.
The dance is wild.
Gubber, forgive me
for swinging out at you.

Forgive me, gubber
for frothing and spewing
dangerously close to your shirt.
You had me pinioned
to limit the damage,
face in the tribal dirt.
And please forgive me
for not really caring
when I started to twitch and convulse
if the thing that kept hitting
the side of my head
was the ground or a policewoman's shoe.
I couldn't help

being dead on arrival.
Gubber, forgive me
for causing a riot
and your face bloodied too.


[1] A word used by Murri and Koori people throughout the east coast of Australia to denote a person of Caucasian race, from a word in the Botany Bay language meaning musket.
[2] A bread baked from strychnine and scone dough.

Toad'n Fess'n Karl went
drinking Friday night.
They looked liked skinheads
in an angry band ex-naval
to the Blundstone bovver boots.
They found a spot of bother
where a gang of cutsnake Kooris
worked to kick an old man's
head in. Instead of kicking heads
they got their heads kicked in.
Toad went down'n Fess went down'n
Karl kept standing up. They kicked them
down but Fess got up again.
Toad could not get up again.
Toad stayed down, stayed dead,
did not get up again. A man
was charged. He broke a policeman's
nose. A murder charge. A black man
on a murder charge. A dead man
on a hero charge. He saved
an old man. Fester
is my brother-in-law'n Karl's
his brother-in-law'n Toad's not
anybody's brother anymore.

professor cockatoo
at the podium
for a little while

in a cloud
of insecticide
falling like flies

kamikaze cries:
beware killer cockatoo
in the box gum tree

eucalyptus splash
on the parquet floor
sweetens teak and pine

professor falling
knocks the podium
into a pine box

tommy gun chatters
kookaburra cackling
long after the joke

no pigeons
no shit on the akubra
at this moment

champagne corks popping
under china
                and mururoa

high on the poop deck
all the shit in the river
cannot touch me

In Brisbane
at the equinox
bats swarm
to the rotting fruit
of Moreton Bay figs.
The dark is half welcome
at the end of summer.
I can run in the park
where Tracey Wiggington
the vampire killer
cut a man's throat
in my favourite place
after offering sex.
The bats squeal protest
as I pass
and shit their seeds
still warm
in splatters
on my neck.

Shaw Neilson bore a saddened axe
towards an assignation
with the eucalypts.
In the Otway Ranges, poverty
took the poet for a paid assassin
contracted to a sawmill
as its musical director.
Neilson shook the handle of the axe
to seal the undertaking.
There would be no supper
until he made it sing.

The forest siren's voice
stole away his resolution.
The axe rusted
as the hungry poet
made his gentle conversation with the trees
listening to the leaves
waiting for the wind.

# *Wild At Heart*

The cassias are all in flower.
Rich dripping juice and yellow blooms
leave streets lined green
with sweating tensions,
smelling of cicadas
in the warming blackness
bursting in.

The invasion of the cassias
leaves poets dripping
shaken citizens
tossing in their sleep exploding images
flowering in their yellow seasons
lining Bramston Terrace.

the hatpin
through the peephole
pierced the voyeur's eye

the waters seep
the shards of galaxies
are lost

the broken organ dries
overdrawn on memories
of dark moondays

when the wetdreams ran
beneath the mask

the hidden rubber sheath
kept moist in dry plastic
moved my love in labour

let her wander
as the high high hem
stiletto high the silksoft
moves through the door to mystery

oh let her come
the eye is opening

Bewitched, Prince Leo Nikolayevich
Myshkin, last and poorest of a line
of noblemen, stares across the room
at her tattooed shoulder, gripped by the itch
to approach her. Nastasya Filippovna gulps her wine
and glances back at him across the room.
Gripped by a fit by the throat in its garrotte,
he falls to the floor and froths, the idiot!

By the time that he comes to, she's gone
and he is lying in his own shit.
After the seizure, his state of mind is one
of insight and shame. (He'll get over it.)
He knows he wants to tell her she has better
tatts than Tank Girl, so he writes her a letter.

Sitting on a ledge above the waves
at Deadman's Beach, he contemplates
the curving of her back and asks:
'How are waves made?  What energy
in that junction of the green sea
with the blue rises to drive them
into curls, catching sun and surfers
with their dissipation into foam?'

He watches the reddening of her neck,
imagining an angry sun beyond content
with browning this sacrifice of skin.
She bares her breasts, turns and asks:
'Will you read that verse to me again?'
He reads, and as he reads, she writes her letter.
'That movie that we saw — *Four Weddings
And A Funeral*... and what was the other one?'

She is adrift.  He turns to the sea again.
The distant blue gives no reward
for watchers for whales, but yesterday
he saw a humpback rise, spout upwards, dive
and leave the spume's illusion stinging
with a question in the corner of his eye.
From where the blue sea turns to green,
the waves roll in.  The surfers break for lunch.

he is certain that his acquisiton
will be better than a lingerie catalogue
but for now he is content to follow her
through the mirrormaze of women's stores
wishing her into the bodysuits
dressing her up in the miniskirts
he cannot afford
                    she is trying
to distort the buckskin
of her own body image
into something that will please him
she is struggling with nausea
creating the sexual persona of bulimia
wishing he would wear it himself

All day she has been smashing bottles.
He walks to her across the shards.

The brown glass bites,
making the meat for the ugly jaws,
the teeth that clamp around the hamburger.

She surrounds herself with glass,
like Briar Rose
comatose
behind the brambles.

He is cutting his feet.

He walks,
anaesthetised by her dead sex.

Infrequently,
the poison lightens.

He wakes from the dream.

She throws another bottle
and the jaws clamp down
like tetanus.

In the garden
in the heartshaped spa
the water is thick
with toadspawn.
I spray the surface
with a film of Mortein,
hoping to deprive the beasts
of oxygen.  The insects die.
The tadpoles swim
more vigorously.

The neighbours' peacock
roosts with its tail
hanging so the feathers drop
on our side of the fence.
The peacock is half mine.

My friend Tony
known as Toad
has never liked his nickname.
He helped me with the Mortein,
recommended chlorine.

A heavy storm
filled the pond again.
The whole neighbourhood croaks.

From the deck
the wet peacock
at twilight
is bedraggled
in silhouette.

On a dry day
I took its feathers
and arranged them in a bottle
empty of the French champagne
that Tony gave us
as a wedding gift.
A peacock feather
signifies death.

This poem
wasn't meant to be a weapon,
but when she reached
to snap an outer petal
from the rose,
the binding fell apart.

The atoms clashed
like crystal knights in tournament,
shattered, sending splinters in
to breach a chain of hearts.

His structure lost,
she wounded,
they are blown apart.

He seeks her now
through all the heart's dark chambers,
stopping now and then
to prise away a thorn.

Across the chasm
breached by fire,
she walks in parallel with him.

They do not coincide.

At the hairdresser
Leanne gets me coffee
and a questionnaire.

I write that people
rarely offer compliments
about my hair.

She cuts it how I like it
the shorter the better
now that I'm going bald

but pushes masculine shampoo
repair conditioner
hair restorer.

Leanne can tell
that I'm a tough customer.

She asks if I believe in UFOs
while she cuts away at my neck
with her cut throat razor.

I tall her the aliens
have used my bald patch
as their launch pad.

Leanne tells me
that she had a bald patch
until she used the hair restorer.

She tells me many women
use the masculine shampoo.

Her hand slices air
with the cut throat razor.

I leave with several
hair care products.

in his empty room
the newly single man
lies awake sweating

the whole building
is full of strange sounds
one sound strikes terror

it is the sound made
by all the single women
whose biological clocks
spring open in unison
crying:  cuckoo!  cuckoo!

These weekend nights
he finds himself
alone in his apartment tower
with city views,
holding himself and rocking
in his black-enamelled
aluminium chair.

Across the balcony
those are the lights
of the university dulled
in this pre-examination week
vacation.  The colleges
are blocks of cells.
He did time there.

The western suburbs lie beyond
and at the horizon, the ranges
where definition is lost.
He watches behind glass doors,
breath misting his reflection
as he runs his fingers back
to find his thinning hair.

On nights like these
he will not venture
to the balcony.
Its pull is sinister
when there are no women below
to cry 'Rapunzel!
Is there room up there?'

## Porn Star Responds To Her Obituary

*for Moana Pozzi*

The best thing about passing on
was not so much the transubstantiation
I had undergone from convent girl
to porn diva, star of Moana, Deep Hole
and on through the final curtain then
to be *L'Espresso's* 'St Moana, Virgin'.
'An Italian icon' said the men
who write for *La Republica.* No!

The best thing was to die at thirty-three,
to die with Popper on the same day
and be the one who boasts the firmer breasts,
the best obituary. The philosopher was miffed
when mine was front page news.
He only made page three.

'But Karl,' I said, 'lie back, relax,
cry *ce l'ho duro!* It's your turn now
to kick your knees up!' Moody bastard
slunk away through a wall, mumbling
something insubstantial about the futility
of trying to dispute a point of reason
with a politician-prostitute. I'd made him
a proposition that he couldn't refute.

'Come Karl, the colour green does not become
a phantom. Dial now, it's not too late
to have some fun.' Hail, Moana, Queen of Heaven!
Memories of me outlive philosophy
with 144 telephone sex lines
still in operation.

*with apologies to Elton John*

I was stalkin' down the street
with my croc suit on
when I saw an alligator
rappin' to a song.
Blastin' down the town
with her ghetto gear
she said 'Croc baby let me
sing it in your ear!'

And this is what she sang:

Urraurra urraurra Reptile Rap!
Urraurra urraurra Reptile Rap!
Teenage mutant ninja turtles
are a lot of crap
when you're hip an' hoppin'
to the Reptile Rap!
Urraurra urraurra Reptile Rap!

Always been a reptile lover
an' I kinda liked her curves.
Went away to think it over.
When I summoned up the nerve
I bought some Lizard condoms
so she wouldn't catch the clap
an' I said 'Gator honey come an'
sit down on my lap!'

And this is what she said:

Urraurra urraurra Reptile Rap!
Urraurra urraurra Reptile Rap!
Teenage mutant ninja turtles
hardly rate a cap
when your heart's a thumpin'
to the Reptile Rap!
Urraurra urraurra Reptile Rap!

Well the years went by
an' ole Croc just died
when the Gator left me
for some snakey guy.
Long nights cryin'
by the condom machine
tryin' to raise the reptile
in my ole blue jeans
while the jukebox played
the Reptile Rap.

With the Crocodile Rock
an' the Reptile Rap
she knocked me back
and she left me flat strap.
Teenage mutant ninja turtles
had to fill the gap
'cos she left me and bereft me
to the Reptile Rap.
Urraurra urraurra Reptile Rap!

I open the elephants' nursery door
and go to the shelves where the nappies are.
I pick up a wrap and a fastener
ready to change little Flora.
There's elephant crap all over the nap.
It's grey and it's sticky and it's slip slop slap.
But that's how it goes when you are an *au pair*
to Queen Celeste and King Babar.
The shite's all right. It's the royals I can't bear
and the regulation palace underwear.
But I had a good time in the cot last night
with Cornelius. He's a bit of all right
with his hoary tusks and his nice firm trunk.
It even stands up when he's roaring drunk.
Though he can't tell love when it butts him in the nuts,
he thinks I only do it for the coconuts.
He thinks I only do it for the coconuts!

I have fallen in love with a photograph
a rollercoaster goddess
in a framer's shop.

She has been hanging there
in fixed ecstasy
since 1946.

Her hair is blonde blown back
by the whizzing rollercoaster
in the anonymous fun park.

You can buy a ticket
but you cannot buy
this woman.

Peaking as the rollercoaster plunges
she half stands
to show her panties and suspenders.

Where the joy is irrepressible
there is no man
except this hidden eye.

The shutter functions
as the painted hands lift high
the short flounced skirt of dreams.

girl in white shorts
rotating on rollerblades
in mannerheim street

girl skates away
as the valio billboard
turns on its axis

face one of the billboard:
a brunette rosebud
dressed in pink silk

face two of the billboard:
full breasts and red roses

face three of the billboard:
rose hips
          and yoghurt

somewhere in helsinki
a girl in white shorts
spins on her rollerblades

summer storm
stars jumping in the pool
their eyes meet

from the mountain
on the toy train
he falls easily

buying beef
the french butcher
thinks they have no brains

she cooks
he chooses wine
carefully

his eyes for her
he turns his back
on french television

Barry Gifford writes of Lula saying:
'Sailor honey, sometimes it seems this world
is turning wild at heart and weird on top.'
Lynch's lens depicts the couple playing
in and out of lingerie.  The world
moves in snakeskin, dancing.  They bop till they drop.
They lack parental guidance, love no laws,
end love sucking Marlboros and Mores.

Slavering beneath repression's skin,
this heart has burst its sheath and wandered wild
and unprotected through that maze of sins
in which the minotaur devours the child,
but given grace in your embrace will stop,
wild at heart, but not so weird on top.

# Power of the Name

My uncle runs a gun shop
in Toowoomba.  In his spare time
he collates the family tree.
On a recent business trip
he found another cousin,
a chicken man in Texas, USA.

Can you see the chickenman
in chickensuit, ten gallon hat
wingtip on the six-gun
struttin' round the chicken ranch
with rootin'-tootin' Uncle Cam
the pistol shootin' gun totin'
mercantile Australian businessman?

Yes, my seventh cousin
is a big American chickenman
with 17 million broody hens
all layin' eggs for
good ol' Uncle Sam.

A postcard from my Uncle Cam
told me of the chickenman.
In my sleep I tossed and cried
that I don't want
to be Kentucky Fried
but Chickenman won't listen
just lifts his leg
and keeps on pissin'
on my uncle's friendly hand.

I had a dream:  it burst
like Woody Allen's old routine:

'Your friend Sam — the one
who thinks he's a chicken,
why did you let them
take him to the asylum?'

'I realised we didn't need the eggs.'

Love comes like a giant chicken
thumbing for a lay
on the road to Austin,
belly swollen with Kentucky Fried,
singing:  I am
the little red rooster.

Love comes like a cock
between the lips
of some poor singer
seeded with dreams
for the vacuum extractor.

I had a dream: it burst
like the egg I fed
into my own insinkerator,
telling Humpty Dumpty
I had a dream.

Every day the chickenman
goes off on his morning rounds,
strutting round the chicken ranch,
wingtip on the trigger
of his huge inseminator,
putting it to all the hens,
even the kitchen supervisor.

Barefoot in the kitchen,
mother hen disturbs her sitting
to go scratching out the worm
of mean existence which
the checkout chick rejects
when the machine fails
at barcode recognition.

Enraged, the mother hen
flies for the machine.  Snatching
the worm from the chick,
she claws the tool and wings it
home.  She hovers over her brood,
reading the barcode too soon
of her offspring's DNA.

The tide turns.  Chickenman returns
like a tired old gun down
to the ebb of his sperm count.
As the swing doors part, the machine
guns him down.  Mother hen turns
from her sitting to stare
at the hate in the eggs

of those barcode eyes
flashing red at the shells
she's warmed, crushing the chicks
without form by premature naming
of trademark names, by the registered
pricing of form, by the terrible
power of the name.

With my feet in the stirrups
riding in the shopfront
of Grandpa Shoesmith's saddlery
all my misgivings
disappeared into the sunset
I imagined on the other side,
on the east side, on the wrong side
of Ruthven Street.

When Grandpa died
the shop passed on to Kevy,
Uncle Kevy who could trade a Chevy
and some opals for a 'dozer
out at Lightning Ridge.
At the end of the dig
he would end the deal
with a half dug shaft
and a battered old Holden utility
into which he piled the whole family
to ride the farm boundary.
With a hand to the brim of his Stetson
he stood and reached for the horizon
saying 'This land, this land
as far as you can see ...'

Uncle Kevy's boys
are selling saddles
in the USA.

This family is a railway siding
and the brothers are chained engines
struggling for the freedom to shunt
up and down the yard for the rest of their lives
hauling their trains of maternal violence,
each day another outburst, another
loosely articulated carriage.

In their children's games
they haul each other round the yard
but they cannot bear to hold each other
and the train derails.
The day is spent filling the bedroom wall
with punched out holes.

They will visit each other sometimes and wish
to rupture all those dark mysteries.
One sees the other's heart as dying tears
that keep his head from bursting bullets.
The other sees his body burned,
his gut a punched out chain.

When I was five
my mother made fantastic
caramel pies
in the new place
on the war service loan
with sliding doors.
She christened
the electric range
by boiling up
condensed milk in a battered
aluminium saucepan
with the handle off.
Within an hour
the Nestle's label
separated from the tin.
The pot boiled dry.
The can went bang —
a gunshot
like her ginger beer exploding.
Like fibreglass
the caramel
stayed on the ceiling.
I took a brush
and painted over it
the day I turned sixteen.

Before I am awake
she has put the child to her elfin breast.
The silken skin does grievous harm.
I up and snatch it way, my child
and take the fierceness of her tears
into another playground where she spills
the Duplo people on the carpet and demands
I build a boat.

Contain the rage, my skin
against the snatching breast my bursting life
would claim my own.  The child is mine.
I snatch it way
to mountain

where the wind is
tiny falling ice.  My sleeping child, I bind her
to my back and walk the Organ Pipes
on Wellington.  The snow turns driving sleet to rain
then back to flaking snow.  A wild joy rises
and I snatch my crying child away
to mother

where she bursts with fretful
joy until the woman leaves again, then flattens.
I set my child an easel and she paints
a muddy rainbow.  Then we walk the dog
until the light fails and the mother's home.
I cook a meal.  She eats it, threatens comfort
so I wrest my child away to bed.
I have a glass of wine.
I nestle to the breast.

Angela is writing a ransom note
to the king of the elves, demanding gold in hoards
in surety for the return of his daughter,
the toothfaerie, her little prisoner.
The local SP bookie is running a tote,
odds on that the note will pluck at his heart, sounding chords
strong enough to make him settle the matter
before the child's human affection can poison her.

I pray that he will not come in the night
and take my daughter away in return for his,
that the faerie repents of withholding rewards to tease
Angela and leaves her the coin that's her right
in exchange for the tooth in the glass, leaving a kiss
of peace on the lips between worlds, winning release.

On the ledge above the beach
my browneyed son torments the waves,
urging them on with stones cast by an arm
just strong enough to send them skimming
from one stone ledge to the next,

bouncing down a step at a time
to where the stairway fails. The stone
skips into the wash of lurching waves,
is dumped and ground on the rocks,
washed over, swallowed and lost

to Joe, who drowns the roar of the waves
with fierce cries and pirate songs,
edging forward on the ledge
to scourge the sea with stones,
falling forward, lurching back when I cry 'No!'

My father woke me in the early hours
to share a view of a total lunar eclipse.
The moon browned quicker than the woman
in the ad for Coppertone.
The window no longer exists.
The house was later smashed for flats.

When I was five we moved to somewhere
stars could easily be seen on moonless nights.
My father named the constellations,
giving me Orion The Hunter
with his great and lesser dogs
to keep me company hunting meteors.

His eyes were sharp enough to differentiate
the blur that was the Pleiades into more
than seven sisters.  He could tell Mars
from Jupiter just by the colour
and identify the South Celestial Pole
by mapping out the Cross and Pointers.

I wondered at the milky rim of galaxy,
read books on amateur astronomy,
absorbed myself in science fiction.
By high school I had mapped the southern sky,
could name each star and planet.  With my telescope
I estimated magnitudes of variable stars.

Plans were made for a bigger instrument.
The components were collected,
but I never finished it.

When I visit my father now he reminds me
of my interest in the stars.  I tell him
that I've lost it.  Until recently he saw
the night sky as a million misty disks
of colour, but they're fading now.  His blindness
on the edge of blackness has eclipsed the sun.

silent white bird
his partner follows
the honk before sunset

absent ibis
kauri pine blackens
sky turns to indigo

black crow shivers
in ibises' flightpath
time for my sweatshirt

On the smoke-scarred mucosa
of his left main bronchus
a wild strain of goblet cells
is beginning to grow,
brewing stringy cupfuls
of mucus and toenails,
hawking like gunmetal
in the back of his throat.

From this hacienda
of industrial anarchy,
cartels are forming
to smuggle out packages
into the bloodstream.
His lymph nodes pay tribute
to a dark mafiosa.

The tulle of illusion
and wonderful plans slip away
when he feels the rock forming
in the angle of his mandible
and the seeds in his liver
grow marble pistachios
that snap the fine metal
of the biopsy needle.

it was when my sons came
that i knew that this shroud
was far too effeminate

why couldn't i be buried
in the same dark suit
as other men?

i left too much of it
up to that woman
i was too reticent
to have my say

so take my power, boys
and take my blessing
i'll take your tears
and your red-eyed rage

and as they lower me
through the mould of my neighbours
i'll take my impotence
into the grave

At the black door,
Father appears
suave and confident.

Will you enter, dreamer?
This house is burning
and Father is the culprit.

Follow him now,
before he vanishes
along the smoke-filled hall.

What's worse:
the panic or the heat?
Father looks confident.

He leads the way to the library
where all the secret books
are stacked
from floor to ceiling.

A sliding panel opens
revealing a leadlined room
with coffins, an examination couch
and a desk with a stethescope.

What about mother?
Flames lap
around the flameproofed room.
Father departs,
looking confident.

The toll of his absence
signals arousal,
awakens Vampira
and several other
sexy sisters of horror.

Somewhere
Mother is burning
and Father is the culprit.

He fails to return
but the hungry girls remain.
The table is laid out
for all the dead pets
of a long childhood.

The feast begins.

A frisky cocker spaniel
chases a thorny devil
up the consulting room curtains.

Now that you are dead, Dad,
it feels like you have no idea
where to put your feet
and your face says
that the sky could come down
to bump you at any moment.

It feels awkward for me, too,
having to lead you about like this,
half wanting to support you,
half wanting to tell you
that you ought to be a man
and stand on your own two feet.

Of course you find it hard
to stay down there, Dad
and I know that you wish
that you could live it all over again,
but I'm taking you back to the grave
where it's cold.  I've got my life to live.

entering the locket
without a photograph
father dreams
the image
of unborn children

their hearts
pitterpatter
in and out
of synchrony

each swallow
of the amnion
each kicking limb
alters the rhythm
of the little drums

they ride
the oscillation
of his thrusts
as mother shudders
drawing breath

# About Interactive Press

Interactive Press is a new Queensland publishing house that seeks to showcase the best contemporary literature by Australian authors. Using emerging technologies, IP will publish in electronic as well as print form. Through its website and links with many online literary sites and services, IP will promote and market its work to the widest possible audience.

Submissions are encouraged, but authors should first obtain guidelines from the IP website, ring us, or contact us by post. *In all correspondence, please enclose a self-addressed stamped envelope — we cannot respond otherwise.*

**Interactive Publications**
9 Kuhler Court
Carindale, Queensland
Australia 4152

Phone/fax (business hours): 61 7 3395-0269
Mobile: 0411-317213
reiter@powerup.com.au
http://www.powerup.com.au/~reiter

## Other Publications Available From Interactive Press

*Hemingway in Spain and Selected Poems* by David P Reiter, 1997, ISBN 0-646-327-46-1, PB, 192 pp, RRP $17.95. Shortlisted for the John Bray Award at the 1998 Adelaide Festival Literary Awards.